KU-510-046

A HISTORY OF BRITAIN

PAPERBIRD

Acknowledgments:
The author and publishers would like to thank Mr Mike Gibson for his help in research, and the following for permission to use illustrative material:
Page 18: Ashmolean Museum, Oxford; cover and 10: Beken of Cowes Ltd; 37: Birmingham Museum and Art Gallery; 34 (centre right): Derbyshire Countryside Ltd; cover and 24: Betty and Nigel Evans; 21, 44: Mary Evans Picture Library; 43: Trevor George; 13: Hulton-Deutsch Collection; 19 (bottom left): is in the custody of the House of Lords Record Office and reproduced by permission of the Clerk of the Records; cover and 27, 29 (centre), 30 (bottom right), 31, 51 (top right): A. F. Kersting; 50: The Master and Fellows, Magdalene College, Cambridge; cover and 21 (centre right): Sylvia Mann; 8, 9, 39: The Mansell Collection; 19 (bottom right), 22, 28, 33 (top right), 45, 47 (top right), 52 (bottom right): Museum of London; 6, 12, 25, 29 (top right), 30 (top left), 36, 49: National Portrait Gallery, London; 35 (bottom left): The National Trust, Cornwall; 23: Peter Newark's Pictures; 16, 17, 47 (top left): Royal Armouries Board of Trustees; 38 (top right): Science Museum, London; 33 (top left), 34 (bottom left), 35 (bottom right): the Victoria and Albert Museum, London; illustrations on pages 6 and 51 by Gavin Young.
Designed by Gavin Young.

British Library Cataloguing in Publication Data
Wood, Tim
    The Stuarts.
    1. England, 1603-1714
    I. Title   II. Dennis, Peter, 1950-   III. Series
    942.06
    ISBN 1-85543-010-X

First edition

Published by Ladybird Books Ltd Loughborough Leicestershire UK
Ladybird Books Inc Auburn Maine 04210 USA
Paperbird is an imprint of Ladybird Books Ltd
© LADYBIRD BOOKS LTD MCMXCI
All rights reserved. No part of this publication may be reproduced, stored in a retrieval system, or transmitted in any form or by any means, electronic, mechanical, photo-copying, recording or otherwise, without the prior consent of the copyright owners.

Printed in England (3)

Contents

The Stuarts

by TIM WOOD

illustrations by PETER DENNIS

Series Consultants: School of History
University of Bristol

Paperbird

The Stuarts

This book covers a period of over a hundred years, during which time there was a bitter struggle between Parliament and the Stuart rulers to decide how the country should be governed. The victory of Parliament made sure that future *monarchs* could not do just as they pleased. Instead they had to govern a *Protestant* United Kingdom through Parliament according to the laws of the land.

Events during Stuart Period

Date	Kings, Queens and people	Events
1600	James I (1603-1625)	
	Guy Fawkes	Gunpowder Plot
		Settlement of Virginia
		'King James' Bible
		Quarrels with Parliament

		Attempt to rule without Parliament 1629-1640
	Charles I (1625-1649)	Quarrels with Parliament 1640-1642
	John Pym	Civil War begins 1642

Oliver Cromwell

New Model Army formed

Battle of Naseby 1645

Charles I captured 1646

Execution of Charles I 1649

1650

Oliver Cromwell
Lord Protector
(1649-1658)

Conquest of Ireland
and Scotland

War against the Dutch

Parliament dismissed

War with Spain

Richard Cromwell
Lord Protector
(1658-1659)

General Monck

Richard quickly overthrown
by the army, which asked
Charles II to return

Charles II
(1660-1685)

Nell Gwyn

Samuel Pepys

Great Plague 1665

Great Fire of London 1666

James II
(1685-1689)

Catholics given important
positions

James flees

William and Mary
(1689-1702)

Bill of Rights 1689

Battle of the Boyne 1690

Bank of England founded

1700

Mary dies 1694

Queen Anne
(1702-1714)

John Churchill,
Duke of Marlborough

War with France. Great
British victories at Blenheim
and Ramillies

1707 Union with Scotland

King James I

When Queen Elizabeth died without any children in 1603, her cousin, James VI of Scotland, became King of England.

James I and VI

James was clever and well educated, but he was not popular. He often said the wrong thing at the wrong time and his thick Scottish accent made him hard to understand. He was also clumsy and even fell down at his own coronation.

During his reign two problems which had been simmering during the Elizabethan Age boiled to the surface. These were the power of Parliament and problems of religion.

A clay pipe as used in Stuart times. James hated smoking and wrote a book in 1604 setting out his arguments against it

James believed that he was king by God's will and he expected Parliament to obey him without question. He entertained so magnificently that he was often short of money. When the MPs refused to vote him any he dismissed Parliament and raised cash by other means, such as by selling land and titles to his friends.

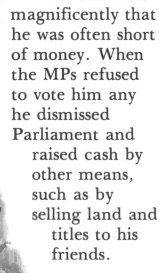

James going to Parliament

James ordered scholars to prepare a new translation of the Bible. The 'King James' Bible was produced in 1611. It was not changed for 300 years and can still be bought today.

The Gunpowder Plot

Soon after James came to the throne, a group of *Roman Catholic* nobles plotted to blow up Parliament. They were angry because James had ordered all Catholic priests to leave the country, and would not allow Catholics to worship as they pleased. They chose a time when the king, the queen and many important nobles and church leaders would be there.

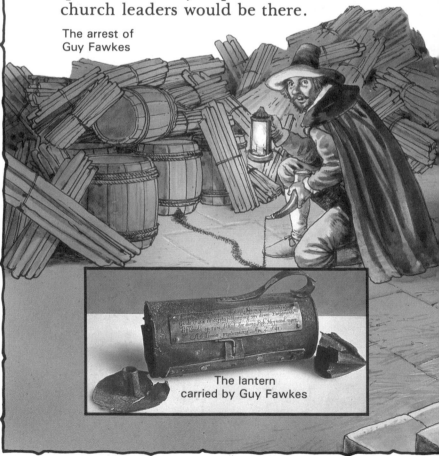

The arrest of Guy Fawkes

The lantern carried by Guy Fawkes

Some historians believe that the king's minister, Robert Cecil, may have known about the plot for a long time. He may have allowed it to go on so that he could catch all the plotters or to make Catholics unpopular throughout the country.

In the early hours of the morning of 5th November 1605 a Catholic soldier, Guy Fawkes, was arrested in a cellar under the House of Lords. He was carrying some matches. Searchers found a tunnel leading from the house next door, and thirty six barrels of gunpowder hidden under a pile of wood in the cellar.

Several other plotters were arrested later. They were all *hung, drawn and quartered*.

Guy Fawkes's usual signature

Guy Fawkes's signature on his confession. It was so shaky because he had been tortured

The Pilgrim Fathers

Like the Catholics, the *Puritans* were not allowed to worship as they wished either. In 1620 some of them decided to sail across the Atlantic and set up a new home in America.

A modern copy of the *Mayflower*. She was less than 30 metres long and 8 metres wide

The Pilgrims called their home
New Plymouth. Friendly North
American Indians taught them
about local plants and seeds

One hundred men, women and children set
out in a ship called the *Mayflower*. After a
stormy voyage lasting sixty seven days, they
landed in America. Although half of them died
during the hard winter, the rest survived to
build a town and start farms.

Charles I

Charles I

In 1625 James died and his son Charles became king. The new king soon quarrelled with Parliament, mainly about money and religion. Charles also believed that he was king by God's will, just as his father had. Parliament tried to use the king's need for money to control his power.

In 1629, Charles decided to rule without Parliament, but his new taxes made him unpopular. In addition, many people feared that Charles would bring back the Roman Catholic religion. This was because he had promised his French wife, Princess Henrietta Maria, that he would do so.

John Pym, the leading opponent of the king

In 1640 Charles, who needed money to fight a war against the Scots, recalled Parliament. MPs, led by John Pym, began to pass laws to control the king. One law said that Parliament could not be dismissed without its own agreement.

In 1642 Charles took an armed guard to Parliament to arrest five of the leading members who opposed him, but they were warned and so escaped. That year, Charles declared war on the Parliamentarians. He left London and headed north to raise an army, calling on all loyal people to support him. Parliament asked its followers to oppose the king. The *Civil War* had begun.

The start of the Civil War

When the Civil War began, people had to choose sides. Sometimes families were bitterly divided in their loyalties, with relations fighting on opposite sides.

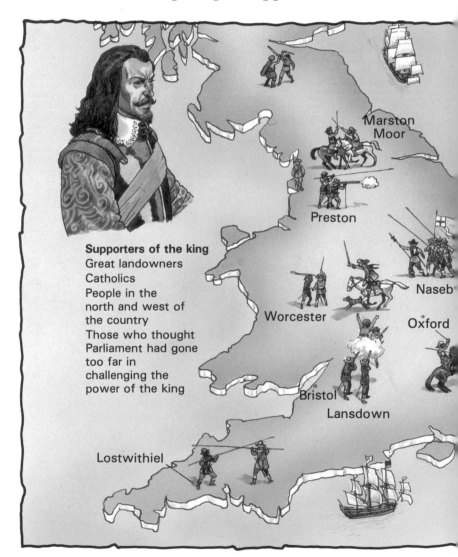

Supporters of the king
Great landowners
Catholics
People in the north and west of the country
Those who thought Parliament had gone too far in challenging the power of the king

Marston Moor

Preston

Naseb

Worcester

Oxford

Bristol

Lansdown

Lostwithiel

Officers in the king's army were called *Cavaliers*. They had long hair and dressed in fine clothes

Soldiers in Parliament's army were called *Roundheads* because of their close cropped hair and round helmets

A Puritan

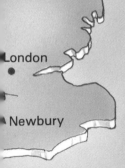

London

Newbury

Supporters of Parliament
Centres of trade and wealth, such as London
Large towns and seaports, whose people hated the king's taxes
Puritans and those who feared the king would bring back the Catholic Church

The triumph of Parliament

After several defeats Parliament appointed a brilliant army captain, Oliver Cromwell, to train its soldiers. He created a 'New Model Army' which crushed the king's army at the battle of Naseby.

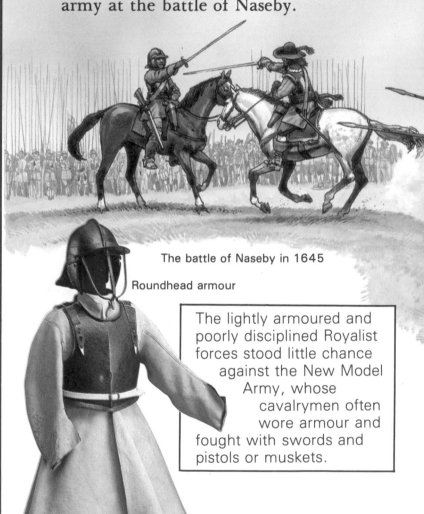

The battle of Naseby in 1645

Roundhead armour

The lightly armoured and poorly disciplined Royalist forces stood little chance against the New Model Army, whose cavalrymen often wore armour and fought with swords and pistols or muskets.

After losing the key towns of Bristol and Oxford, Charles surrendered. Parliament could not decide what to do with him. In 1648 Charles escaped from London and tried to restart the war. Cromwell believed that as long as Charles lived, there would never be peace in the land. He decided to arrest the king and put him on trial for *treason*.

The New Model Army

A sword used in the Civil War

Pikes, which were 6 metres long, formed a steel hedge around the army

Muskets were heavy and clumsy but the bullets could pierce armour

The execution of the king

In 1649 the real power in the country was the army. MPs who still wished to make a pact with the king were driven out of Parliament. Those who remained prepared for the king's trial in Westminster Hall.

Throughout his trial Charles behaved with great dignity. He refused to accept that the court had any right to try him. He was called a *tyrant*, a traitor and a murderer, and sentenced to death.

John Bradshaw, the president of the court, wore this steel-lined hat for protection against attack

It was a freezing day in January when Charles went to the *scaffold*. He wore an extra shirt so that he would not shiver and seem afraid. After making a short speech he laid his head on the block. A loud groan rose from the crowd as the executioner's axe came down.

Part of Charles's death warrant

The extra shirt Charles wore

Witchcraft

In Stuart times people believed that witches were working with the devil to try to harm good people. If someone died or a cow went sick for no apparent reason, it was easy to blame a witch.

Most people were so frightened by being arrested that they

Suspected witches were often 'floated'. They were lowered into water. If they floated, they were witches. If they sank they were innocent, but probably died by drowning!

confessed they were witches and often gave away others. Witches were hanged. We will never know how many innocent people, mostly old women, died for the sake of this terrible superstition.

People with pets were instantly suspected because witches were thought to keep their own evil spirit in an animal called a *familiar*, which they fed on their blood. Witch finders looked for a strange mark on the body from which the familiar drank blood. They also searched for a witch mark, a spot on the body where a pin could be pushed in, causing no bleeding or pain.

My Imps names are

1 Ilemauzar
2 Pyewackett

Images from a book on witchcraft showing Matthew Hopkins *(top right)* who was called the 'Witch Finder General'

Cromwell throwing out the MPs in 1653

The Commonwealth

After the execution of the king Britain became a *republic*, called the *Commonwealth*, ruled by Cromwell and Parliament. However, when Parliament would not agree to new *elections*, Cromwell, backed by the army, dismissed the MPs and ruled, as Lord Protector, himself.

Cromwell's *death mask*. He died in 1658. While he was Lord Protector he was paid £100,000 a year.

Things forbidden by the Puritans

Life under the Commonwealth was shaped by the Puritans. Laws were passed against swearing, dancing, card playing and football. Theatres and inns were closed. No one was allowed to work on Sundays. At one stage even Christmas dinner was forbidden. Many people hated these laws and longed for a return to things as they used to be.

Puritans. They believed in a simple life and hard work

The merry monarch

When Cromwell died in 1658 his son, Richard, became Lord Protector. He was disliked by the army and soon retired. An army officer, General Monck, who realised that Britain had to have a ruler, invited Charles I's son to return from abroad to become King Charles II.

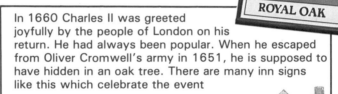

ROYAL OAK

In 1660 Charles II was greeted joyfully by the people of London on his return. He had always been popular. When he escaped from Oliver Cromwell's army in 1651, he is supposed to have hidden in an oak tree. There are many inn signs like this which celebrate the event

Charles II loved dancing and the theatre. He held magnificent balls and banquets. His expensive court and costly wars against the Dutch meant that he was always short of money.

Since Parliament did not like to grant him taxes, Charles had to turn to the French King Louis XIV for money. It was given to him in return for promising to bring back the Roman Catholic Church to Britain, although Charles did not actually do this.

Charles II

The Great Plague

The summer of 1665 was unusually hot. During June a terrible plague struck London killing 68,000, a quarter of the people who lived there. The filthy, narrow streets provided perfect conditions for the rats to breed and for the disease to spread.

Carters toured the streets ringing bells and shouting, 'Bring out your dead.' They took the corpses out of the town, buried them in a pit and covered them with *quicklime*.

Red crosses were painted on the doors of houses which had been visited by the plague. The people inside were not allowed to come out. Sometimes food was left for them on the doorstep.

Plague gateway built after an earlier plague in London's Seething Lane where the famous diarist Samuel Pepys lived

There was no cure for the plague. Some thought it was caused by foul air so fires were lit in the streets to drive it away. Many people fled to the countryside to escape.

Searchers of the dead would visit any house where there had been a death to see if it had been caused by plague. Doctors wore special hoods with beaks. There were herbs in the beaks to filter the air

Like the Black Death in 1348, the plague was carried by fleas that lived on rats

The Great Fire of London 1666

In the year following the plague, a second disaster struck London. A fire broke out in a baker's shop in Pudding Lane. Fanned by a strong wind, the flames spread quickly through the narrow streets of wooden houses.

Primitive fire fighting equipment like this was not much use

Many people panicked and, grabbing what belongings they could carry, fled for the river Thames

Samuel Pepys. He was in London at the time. He wrote in his diary that he buried some expensive wine and a large cheese in his garden before fleeing.

The Monument. It was built where the Great Fire started

The king ordered sailors to blow up houses with gunpowder in order to make an open space across which the fire could not cross. But it was not until the fifth day of the fire, when the wind changed direction, that the flames were at last brought under control. Much of London was left a charred and smoking ruin.

Sir Christopher Wren, Surveyor-General to the king

Sir Christopher Wren

So much of London had been destroyed by the Great Fire that the king called on the architect, Christopher Wren, to design a new city.

St Paul's Cathedral. Wren rebuilt fifty one churches, but the cathedral was his masterpiece. It took thirty seven years to build. Wren was buried there when he died aged ninety.

Many of Wren's plans were never carried out because people often preferred to build their new houses and shops on the sites of the old ones. However, Wren did make sure that all buildings in the city were built of stone or brick and that roads were made wider. He left behind him a healthier and more beautiful capital city.

Inside St Stephen's Walbrook Church, London, designed by Wren

What people ate

The food of most people changed little from Tudor times. Bread, cheese, cheap cuts of meat and beer remained the main items on the menu.

lamb · roast chicken · roast beef · fruit and cheese · rabbit stew · pheasant · wine · oysters · fruit tart · lobster

Samuel Pepys wrote in his diary that on one occasion he gave his guests this meal

Wealthy people ate huge amounts of meat, poultry and fish. Increasing trade with overseas countries brought new kinds of food from abroad, such as tomatoes, pineapples, cauliflowers and chocolate.

Dinner guests brought their own spoons or one of the new forks that were coming into use

A tea caddy. Tea was so expensive that it was kept locked up

Coffee houses became very popular in Charles II's reign. Merchants and scholars went to them to discuss business, to hear newspapers read aloud or just to talk. They drank coffee, chocolate, or a new and very expensive drink from India called tea.

a coffee pot of the time

Homes

The houses of rich nobles and merchants were more comfortable than they had been in Tudor times. They were built of stone or brick with sash windows and a regular shape.

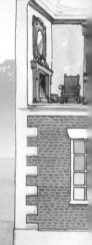

Four poster beds became very popular. This one can be seen at Chatsworth House

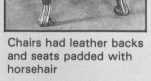

Chairs had leather backs and seats padded with horsehair

Each room now had its special purpose and bathrooms were beginning to appear by the end of the period.

Inside, walls were often covered with wooden panelling

Doors and staircases were skilfully carved by craftsmen

Clocks were much more accurate. Many chimed the hours

Cupboards were used instead of chests for storing clothes

James II

James II

When Charles II died in 1685, his brother succeeded him and became King James II. He was a Catholic and soon began to put Catholics in positions of power in the army and in the government. This worried many leading Protestants and when James had a son to start a line of Catholic kings, they decided to make sure this would not happen.

Protestant rebels, led by the Duke of Monmouth in 1685, were defeated at the battle of Sedgemoor. Judge Jeffreys was sent to punish them. At the 'Bloody *Assizes*' he brutally condemned two hundred to be hanged and eight hundred to be sold as slaves to the West Indies. Monmouth was executed.

They offered the crown to Mary, James's Protestant daughter and her husband William, the Dutch Protestant leader. William and Mary landed at Torbay and James marched to attack them. When his army and his generals began to desert, James lost the will to fight and fled to France. Parliament offered the throne jointly to William and Mary.

William and Mary coronation plate

James fled by boat. He threw the *Great Seal* into the Thames hoping that William and Mary would have problems ruling without it.

Science

Before the Stuart Period little was known about science and a great deal of what *was* known was based on guesswork or superstition.

An early microscope developed by Robert Hooke, a brilliant scientist of the time

During James I's reign Roger Bacon began to carry out scientific experiments to discover more about the world.

In 1665, Isaac Newton discovered the law of gravity by watching an apple fall from a tree. He went on to put forward other important laws about motion. Much of modern science is based on his ideas.

In 1628 William Harvey wrote a book explaining how the heart is a pump for moving blood round the body. Many people thought he was mad.

Roger Bacon's ideas about the importance of experiments were continued by scientists throughout Stuart times and as a result some very exciting discoveries were made. By the end of the period more was known about the human body, nature and the planets than ever before, although not everyone believed these new ideas.

Better instruments like this telescope helped scientists to make more accurate observations

Charles II took a keen interest in science. He founded a club called the Royal Society where leading doctors, scientists and astronomers could discuss their work.

What people wore

During the early Stuart Period fashions became more colourful. Clothes lost the padded stiffness of the Elizabethan Age and became looser. Ribbons became popular decorations.

Cavalier about 1630

wide brimmed hat

long hair

soft collar

high waisted suit

cuff turned back

breeches below the knee

short cloak

A lady about 1645

masks were sometimes used to protect skin from sun

deep lace collar

full skirt

expensive silk petticoat

Puritan about 1655

wide brimmed hat

plain collar

short coat

Puritan wife about 1655

deep linen collar

very simple hairstyle under a linen cap

brown woollen dress

wide linen cuff turned back

linen apron

Gentleman about 1690

full wig

short jacket with open sleeves

lace cuffs

silk stockings

high heeled shoes with ribbons

Then, during the Commonwealth, fashions became simpler, because most forms of decoration were banned. When Charles II became king, colour and decoration returned, with many fashions brought from France where Charles had lived during Cromwell's rule.

Lady about 1690

loose, flowing hair

wide sleeves

silk overdress

skirt pulled back

underskirt in a different colour

Colonies and trade

Throughout the Stuart Period, the eastern coast of America was settled by the British. The early *pioneers* had a very hard time but eventually they set up colonies which prospered through fishing, fur trapping and tobacco growing.

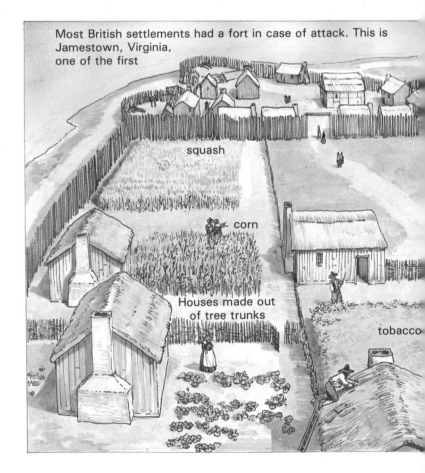

Most British settlements had a fort in case of attack. This is Jamestown, Virginia, one of the first

squash

corn

Houses made out of tree trunks

tobacco

Bristol docks. Bristol became an important trading port in Stuart times

British ships traded all over the world, bringing back goods such as sugar and *indigo* from the West Indies. People put money into trading companies, like the East India Company, sure that they would make big profits.

One of the Nails in Bristol. Trading was done near these and then merchants paid 'on the nail'

People at work

Most people still worked on the land in Stuart times, but industry was becoming more important. Wool was spun and woven in most country cottages.

spinning wheel

Merchants called clothiers bought the wool, took it to the cottages and paid for the finished cloth.

The fastest growing industry was coal. Coal was carried by sea from Newcastle to heat homes in London. Hundreds of small boys worked in the capital climbing and sweeping chimneys.

a wine bottle made in 1665

The iron industry, glass making and salt mining were also important. Ships built in ports like Newcastle and Bristol carried the goods overseas.

Travelling around

Roads in Stuart Britain were very bad. The people in each *parish* were supposed to repair the roads, but since the work was unpaid it was not often done. As a result the roads were full of ruts and holes. Stagecoaches often overturned or became stuck.

Another danger to travellers came from highwaymen

Stagecoaches first appeared in Stuart times. They were very slow and uncomfortable. Passengers stayed overnight in coaching inns.

Travellers held up with a pistol like this had to pay with their money or their lives

Streets in towns were very dirty. The rich were often carried in sedan chairs like this one

Some roads had *toll* gates where travellers had to pay

Postboys carried the Royal Mail. In 1640 it took ten days to send a letter from London to Edinburgh.

Rich people usually had their own carriages

The quickest and safest way to travel was often by water. Goods travelled by barge along the rivers and the Thames was like a main highway.

The last of the Stuarts

When William and Mary came to the throne in 1689, Parliament drew up a list of rules to control their power. This list was called the Bill of Rights. When William signed the Bill, Parliament finally won the great struggle which had gone on throughout the Stuart Period to decide whether Parliament or the king was more powerful.

Bill of Rights
1689

1 Parliament will decide on all laws and taxes.

2 The King must be a Protestant.

3 No one can go to prison without a trial.

4 Parliament will decide on whether there will be an army.

William used the British army and navy to defend his native Holland against the French king, Louis XIV

Queen Anne and her ministers

When William died in 1702, James II's other daughter Anne became queen. During her reign Scotland was united with the rest of Britain and Members of Parliament began to divide into two parties, the *Whigs* and the *Tories*.

Queen Anne was the last of the Stuarts. She had sixteen children but they all died. When she herself died in 1714, Parliament decided to offer the throne to a Protestant German, Prince George, who was the great grandson of James I. A new Georgian Age was about to begin.

Anne's general, John Churchill, Duke of Marlborough, won a series of brilliant victories against the French

ROMANS 700BC – AD383	SAXONS AND NORMANS 383 – 1272	MIDDLE AGES 1272 – 1485	TUDORS 1485 – 1603

1083 yrs > 889 yrs > 213 yrs > 118 yrs >

TIMELINE GUIDE TO *A HISTORY OF BRITAIN*

How we know

The events in this book happened over two hundred and fifty years ago – so how do we know about them?

Historians use EVIDENCE, rather like detectives do, to piece a story together.

Some BOOKS describing Stuart times have survived to this day. One of the best known is the diary of Samuel Pepys in which he describes life in London during the reign of Charles II.

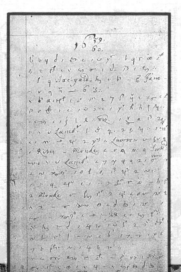

A page from Pepys's diary. He wrote it in a shorthand code he invented

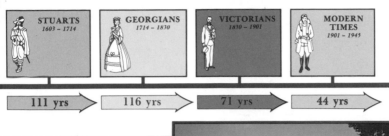

| STUARTS 1603 – 1714 | GEORGIANS 1714 – 1830 | VICTORIANS 1830 – 1901 | MODERN TIMES 1901 – 1945 |

| 111 yrs | 116 yrs | 71 yrs | 44 yrs |

Blenheim Palace. Given to the Duke of Marlborough as a reward for his victory at the battle of Blenheim

There are still a lot of BUILDINGS such as Blenheim Palace shown here that have survived to this day. A list of places to visit is on page 56.

Archaeologists have EXCAVATED many Stuart sites. OBJECTS found by archaeologists are often stored in museums. Although many of the objects are metal, stone or pottery we do have more delicate objects made from wood, cloth, and even glass, such as Samuel Pepys's spectacles. There is a list of museums to visit on page 56.

Some of these old objects dating from Stuart times seem strange to us. What do you think this is? You will find the answer on page 56

51

The legacy of the Stuarts

The Stuart Age brought great changes. The uniting of England and Scotland in 1707 meant that people now talked about the two countries as Great Britain. The religious quarrels that had troubled the Tudors were largely settled, and Britain was now firmly a Protestant country.

The triumph of Parliament in the Civil War laid the foundations of a parliamentary system of government which later became a model for other countries. Britain had achieved success in trading and fighting abroad. She was poised to become an important world power.

Inventions and discoveries

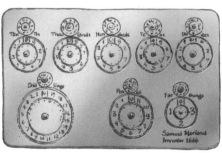

calculators

grandfather clocks

chocolate

coffee

tea

circulation of the blood

steam engines

using coal to smelt iron

A Dutchman,
Dirck Hartog, was the
first European to land on
Australian soil in 1616

Glossary

assizes: law courts for trying important cases throughout the counties

Catholic: see Roman Catholic

Cavalier: a supporter of the king in the Civil War

Civil War: a war fought by the citizens of the same country

Commonwealth: a state in which the whole people have a voice and an interest

death mask: a wax impression of the face of a dead person

election: choosing members of Parliament by voting

familiar: a companion spirit

Great Seal: the stamp which was pressed onto hot wax to leave an impression. It was used to seal the most important documents which were issued in the name of the monarch

hung, drawn and quartered: a method of execution where criminals were first hanged, then had their vital organs removed and their bodies cut into four parts

indigo: a blue dye extracted from the indigo plant

monarch: a king or queen

parish: a district with its own church and clergyman

pioneer: someone who goes first to prepare the way for others

Protestant: a Christian not of the Catholic or Orthodox Churches

Puritan: Protestants who believed in simple services and plain churches

republic: a country without a monarch that is ruled entirely by Parliament

Roman Catholic: a member of the Church of Rome

Roundheads: supporters of Parliament in the Civil War. They were called this because of their short haircuts and round helmets, which made them look as if they had round heads

quicklime: a white powder which burns away flesh

scaffold: a platform built for an execution

scrofula: a disease of the glands which causes swelling, ulcers and itching

taxes: compulsory charges paid to the government

toll: a charge paid by travellers for using a road or bridge

Tories: members of one of the main political parties in Britain during the Stuart and later periods. Tories originally opposed those who wanted to stop any Catholic becoming monarch

treason: acting against your own country

tyrant: a cruel ruler

Whigs: members of one of the main political parties in Britain during the Stuart and later periods. Whigs originally wanted to prevent any Catholic becoming monarch

Index

Places to visit

HOUSES, CASTLES AND PALACES

Ashdown House, near Newbury, Berkshire
Blenheim Palace, Woodstock, Oxfordshire
Blickling Hall, near Aylsham, Norfolk
Bourne Mill, Colchester, Essex
Drumlanrig Castle, Thornhill, Dumfriesshire
Eyam plague village, near Bakewell, Derbyshire
Gladstone's Land, Edinburgh
Ham House, Richmond, London
Hatfield House, Hertfordshire
Milton's Cottage, Chalfont St Giles, Buckinghamshire
Museum of the History of Science, Broad Street, Oxford
Pitstone Post Mill, Ivinghoe, Buckinghamshire
Sudbury Hall, near Uttoxeter, Derbyshire
Wilton House, near Salisbury, Wiltshire
Woolsthorpe Manor, Colsterworth, near Grantham, Lincolnshire

MUSEUMS

Most city museums will have objects from this period. Especially good collections can be seen at:

Cromwell's Museum, Huntingdon, Cambridgeshire
Old Royal Observatory, Greenwich Park, London
National Maritime Museum, Greenwich
Science Museum, South Kensington, London
Tower of London, Tower Hill, London

The object on page 51 is a gold 'touchpiece' of about 1680. They were given to people who had been touched by the king. These people had the disease *scrofula*. It was thought that being touched by a king would cure them